7.99

About this book

Tigers are now on the verge of extinction. Perhaps the most handsome of the big cats, they have been mercilessly hunted and their territory gradually reduced as people's need for agricultural land has increased. Cathy Kilpatrick describes the lives of these shy and largely solitary animals — their adaptation to snow and jungle, their hunting techniques, their prowess as swimmers, and their sometimes deserved reputation as man-eaters.

About the author

Cathy Kilpatrick is a zoologist and a freelance writer and broadcaster. Her travels have taken her to Australia to study locusts and to many areas of Europe, Japan and Africa. In 1978 she and her husband were chosen by the BBC to make a film about the wildlife of north Queensland as an entry for the Mike Burke Award. She has written many books on zoology, including several for children, and is the compiler of "Two by Two", a radio quiz program about animals.

Sir Maurice Yonge, Consultant Editor to the series, is Honorary Fellow in Zoology in the University of Edinburgh.

Animals of the World

First published in 1980 by
Wayland Publishers Limited
49 Lansdowne Place, Hove
East Sussex, BN3 1HF, England

Typesetting in the U.K. by Granada Graphics
Printed in Italy by G. Canale & C. S.p.A., Turin

First published in the United States of America by
Raintree Publishers Limited, 1980

Library of Congress Cataloging in Publication Data

Kilpatrick, Cathy.
  Tigers

  (Animals of the world)
  Includes index.
  SUMMARY: Text and photographs introduce the
characteristics, habits, and habitat of tigers.
    1. Tigers—Juvenile literature. [1. Tigers]
1. Title. 11. Series.
QL737.C23K54 1980   599'.74428   79-19112
  ISBN 0-8172-1088-1 lib. bdg.

Animals of the World
Consultant Editor: Sir Maurice Yonge CBE FRS

Tigers

Cathy Kilpatrick

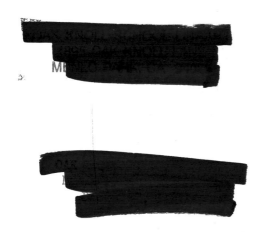

🔴 RAINTREE CHILDRENS BOOKS
Milwaukee • Toronto • Melbourne • London

With its rich orange brown fur and its fine black stripes the tiger is the most distinctive, and many people think the most handsome, of all the big cats. There is a good deal of white fur, too, on the insides of the legs, the belly and the area around the face. The tiger is also fierce and strong — its body is long, narrow and lithe with very powerful muscles in the massive forelimbs which give it great strength.

Tigers' faces are most beautifully marked. Each has its own individual pattern, just as human faces vary from person to person. In fact, people studying tigers in the wild can recognize individual animals by looking at their faces. The large eyes are on the front of the head, so that tigers have binocular vision and can judge distances very accurately. This is important when they are hunting, for they need to see ahead clearly. Because of the position of the eyes, tigers cannot see all around themselves. But since they do not need to protect themselves from enemies (except people) this is not a disadvantage for them.

Tigers have very good hearing. Their ears are used for another purpose too: they show the animal's moods and feelings. Pricked ears mean the tiger is alert and listening. When the ears are laid back flat, the tiger is contented and lying still. The white spot on the back of each ear can be seen from some distance away. This enables the tiger to signal to other tigers and cubs (*right*).

The tiger has a good sense of smell, but not as good as that of the wild dogs that are the tiger's distant cousins. Its whiskers are used to help it find its way in the jungle. These long, strong hairs are sensitive to touch, which is particularly useful when the tiger is moving around in dim light. They help the tiger to feel what it cannot see clearly, in the way a cane helps a blind person.

It is incorrect to think of the tiger as living only in the hot, steamy tropical rain forests of India and southeast Asia. Tigers do live in these places, but they can also be found in some areas that are very cold and snowy (*above*). In fact, the tigers' ancestors originally came from an extremely cold area: northern Siberia. A small number of Siberian tigers still live there. They have longer fur than tigers living in warmer regions, and they have more fat on their bodies to help keep them warm. They have been

seen roaming abroad in the hardest frosts, even in temperatures as low as $-35°C$ ($-30°F$). The Siberian tiger is not the only kind of tiger that lives in cold regions. Indian and Chinese tigers can also live in the snowy landscapes of high mountains.

This Siberian tiger (also called the Amur or Manchurian tiger) is much more powerfully built than any other tiger. The old males have massive shoulders and huge heads. From the nose to the tip of the extended tail they measure on average about

3 m. (10 ft.), although some hunters in the nineteenth century reported killing tigers considerably larger than this. Despite legal protection, today there are only about 150 Siberian tigers left in the Soviet Far East. Most of these live in the reserves north of Vladivostok. The Chinese report that a few still live under protection in northeast China.

Today the tiger species, *Panthera tigris*, is divided into eight races, or sub-species. Most are on the verge of extinction or already extinct. This is partly because tigers have always been regarded as savage and fierce and so they have been the hunter's most prized trophy. Another reason for the decreasing number of tigers is that much of their habitat has now been destroyed to make room for farmland and agriculture.

Of the eight races, three were found on islands. The Bali tiger, however, is now extinct — although it was still common on the island in 1914. In 1937 the last one was reported to have been shot. Tigers are still found on the island of Java, to the west of Bali. The Java tiger, however, is on the brink of extinction. It seems there are only

four or five survivors in the wild. There are
no Java tigers in zoos, either.

On the much larger island of Sumatra,
which lies to the northwest of Java, the tiger
is a little more numerous. There are possibly
about 1,000 tigers of the Sumatran race still
alive. This is a handsome specimen in the
photograph. The Javan and Sumatran tigers

tend to be smaller than those on the mainland. They are generally darker in color and have narrower, closer, stripes. The Sumatran race also has less white fur.

Illegal hunting is still taking place openly in Sumatra. Unless this is stopped and the existing protective laws firmly enforced, the Sumatran tiger, too, may face extinction. Fortunately there are Sumatran tigers in several zoos around the world, where they are being bred successfully. In this photograph a young cub is being fed in a zoo hospital. Breeding programs in zoos may allow certain races of tiger to be re-introduced into the wild. In captivity even weaklings may survive with extreme care and hand-rearing by devoted zoo staff.

The Caspian tiger once lived in Afghanistan, Iran, Iraq, Turkey and the Soviet Union. It, too, is feared to be extinct.

The World Wildlife Fund launched "Operation Tiger" in the 1970s. It provided equipment and scientific assistance for tiger conservation in Bangladesh, Bhutan, India, Nepal, Thailand, and southeast Asia. By 1979 the number of tigers was thought to be increasing, especially in India and Nepal.

Over 2,000 Indian tigers survive in the wild today. A fine specimen can be seen on the left. In other areas the tiger, hopefully, will survive.

Above are white, or albino, tigers. They are born without any orange brown color in their fur. Most albino animals have pinkish eyes, but white tigers have beautiful icy, blue green eyes. People have always found these tigers especially fascinating. One was caught and taken to England to be shown to the public as long ago as 1820.

In 1952 a white male cub was caught in the Rewa forest in India. A local maharajah kept it on the grounds of his palace. When it was adult it was mated with a normal female which produced four white cubs with blue eyes. More white tigers were born in later breedings. The Indian Government decided to share these beautiful animals with the rest of the world. Some of the offspring can be found as prized exhibits in a number of Indian, European and North American zoos. Some of the zoos, such as Bristol Zoo in England, have bred their own white tigers.

The tiger's striped coat provides excellent camouflage in the wild, for tigers often live in areas where there is tall grass or jungle undergrowth. When hiding in this vegetation, the tiger blends perfectly with its surroundings. The white on the face, chest and legs also helps to break up the animal's outline so that it is more difficult to see. The tiger in the photograph on pp. 12-13 is well hidden. It can safely scan the land for prey.

In the wild the tiger and tigress live separate lives for most of the time. During the day a tiger spends a great deal of time resting or sleeping, hidden in the dappled

light and foliage of the jungle. This huge cat is very lazy, only occasionally lifting its head to look around, sniff the air or take a big yawn. When in deep sleep, a tiger will roll on its back, open its mouth wide and breathe heavily.

In very hot weather, and especially in the intense heat of midday, the tiger loves to swim. Sometimes it flings itself into the water, appearing to enjoy the terrific belly-flop and splash. It closes its eyes as it hits the water.

At other times the tiger wades slowly into a stream, pool or slow-flowing river. It will then sit for some time with only its shoulders and head out of the water. Observers

have noticed that a tiger sitting in water hides from Indian elephants which pass close by or drink from the water. One tiger sank its whole head and body into a thick growth of reeds and water lilies until only its nose and eyes were visible. It stayed perfectly still until the elephants had gone away. Other tigers have been seen scooping water over their bodies, using their front paws.

18

In the colder, northern parts of its range the tiger does not have these problems with the heat, but the mosquitoes and midges are a great nuisance in the short summer. They bite and annoy the Siberian tiger so that it will often seek refuge in the spray of a waterfall where the insects do not fly.

The tiger is an excellent swimmer. This is one reason why it is found over such a wide area, for broad rivers and lakes did not stop it crossing into new lands when it spread from its original northern home. When swimming, the tiger's head and neck are above the water, with just the tip of its long tail breaking the surface.

Often, the tiger leaves the water and goes to a sheltered spot. Slowly but surely it then grooms its fur, using its tongue to sleek its coat — just like a pet cat cleaning itself. The tiger also washes its face in just the same way as a cat: first it licks its paw, then it wipes its face with the paw.

The tiger is a shy animal, wandering alone in the jungles and forests. It usually hunts during the hours of darkness, although it may begin its search in the late afternoon or around dusk. It walks slowly

through the forest in search of prey, keeping its ears pricked for unusual sounds that may betray a victim (*right*). Each tiger establishes regular paths and routes in its own particular area of jungle (*below*).

Because it does not live in large groups and does not move around much during the day, the tiger is very difficult to study in the wild. However, even in dense jungle one can tell when a tiger has been nearby. Huge,

long scars can be found on the bark of trees where the tiger regularly sharpens its claws. Its paw prints (pugmarks) can also be seen when the ground is soft. This photograph shows some pugmarks. The larger print is a front paw; the smaller one is a hind paw.

A male tiger will stop and sniff a tree or bush. Then, every so often, it will spray the tree or bush to mark out its territory. It lifts its tail, curls it over its back, and shoots out a jet of urine.

These markings tell any other male tiger that enters the area that the territory is already occupied. The strong smell also lets a tigress know that a male is living in the area.

A tigress that is ready to mate will also leave its sign by squirting sprays of urine and leaving droppings at certain spots. This tells a male entering her territory that she is ready to mate. Sometimes a tiger stops and lets out a loud roar, to let other tigers know

that it occupies that area.

As the tiger moves through the forest, the birds let forth their alarm cries, the monkeys squeal in warning and the squirrels chatter and scamper away. The jungle tiger's favorite prey is the wild pig of central and southeast Asia, and various kinds of deer.

In India, the two kinds of deer most often killed are the chital or axis deer, and the barasingha or marsh deer. The chital is a handsome, spotted deer. The male has very

large antlers. The barasingha deer looks like the red deer of Europe and Asia. Another deer eaten by the tiger is the sambar, which is found from China to Ceylon. This is the largest of the deer which are found in southeast Asia.

When it sees a deer, the tiger freezes. The huge cat drops down until its belly hugs the ground. Slowly it begins to slink forwards. Each time the deer lifts its head the tiger stops dead in its tracks. Its camouflage and

perfect stillness usually prevent it from being seen, so it can get very close to its prey. As the tiger crouches it judges the exact distance to its intended victim (*above*).

When the tiger is ready for the final attack it flattens its body to the ground and remains absolutely motionless. Even its long tail is perfectly still. At other times, such as when the tiger is sleeping or resting, the tail moves. This movement might warn other animals of the tiger's presence.

As the tiger gets ready to spring, the muscles in its legs tighten. A quiver runs along the length of its body to the tip of the flattened tail. Then the tiger springs and lands on the deer. The full force of the impact knocks the deer off balance. Using one of its large forepaws, the big cat forces the victim's head up and sinks its teeth into the neck. It does not let go until the deer has stopped breathing. The tiger's teeth and jaws are so strong that the bones of the deer's neck are often broken and the windpipe and gullet cut right through.

Whenever possible, a tiger approaches its prey under the cover of grass or bushes. If its prey is feeding in the open, however, the tiger has to break out of cover. It rushes towards its victim, seizes it with sharp claws, quickly takes it by the throat and brings it to the ground.

When the prey has been killed, the tiger usually drags or carries the carcass to a secluded place. Often this is a thicket near water. The cat usually grasps the prey by the neck and drags it along between its forelimbs or beside its body.

No matter what time of the day it is, the

tiger then begins to feed. Usually it prefers to feed at the rump of larger victims, such as deer, antelope or cattle. With smaller prey, such as a pig, it often begins at the head. The tiger's cheek teeth — called carnassial teeth — are most important in feeding. When the lower jaw is brought up to meet the upper jaw these sharp teeth pass close to each other like the blades of a pair of scissors. This makes them highly efficient cutting tools. They slice the skin and meat

into easily-swallowed lumps. The front paws are used to hold a part of the victim's body while the teeth tear into it.

A tiger will usually eat voraciously for about an hour or so before taking a rest. It devours the skin with the meat, except for that on the head and lower parts of the leg. A tiger can eat a pig or a large chital stag in one day, a sambar antelope in two days, or a buffalo in three days.

The tiger swallows all the small bones of its prey. The larger bones are sometimes propped between the pads of the forepaws and gnawed, in the way a pet dog eats a bone (*above*). If the tiger is eating at night, it tries to drag the carcass to better cover as dawn approaches. If it is going to leave some to eat later, it hides the kill or covers it over with leaves and grasses.

From time to time while it is eating or

resting, a tiger goes to a nearby stream to quench its thirst. Usually it crouches with its head lowered between the slightly parted forepaws. It laps the water just as a cat laps eagerly at a saucer of milk. It can drink for two minutes without stopping. Sometimes the tiger walks into the water up to its belly to drink. Occasionally it will immerse itself up to its eyes, blowing and spluttering. One naturalist observing tigers in the wild records how he saw a tiger put its muzzle underwater and begin to chomp strongly. He believed the tiger was giving itself this mouthwash to clean its teeth.

The tiger appears to kill prey only when it is hungry. However, some tigers have become known as "man-eaters" and "killers." This has led to tigers being shot by the thousands. Over most of the tiger's range, however, man-eaters are rare. India is famous for its supposed man-eating tigers. In 1902, a total of 1,046 persons were listed by the Indian government as having been killed by tigers.

A tiger turns to killing people when its normal pattern of hunting for food has broken down. A tiger that has been wounded

by hunters is unable to pursue and catch wild animals. It may first take domestic cattle from local villages and then turn on the villagers themselves. Older, weaker tigers have found killing cattle, or humans, an easier way of obtaining food. With age, a tiger's sharp teeth (*left*) can become worn and broken. It cannot move as fast as it could when it was younger. So it is driven by hunger to catch easy meals: a human being is even easier to knock down and kill than a domestic cow.

In the past, man-eating tigers terrorized villagers in parts of India. Some villages had high fences built round the groups of huts because some tigers were so bold that they would enter the village, break into a hut and drag a villager away. Occasionally a whole village would be moved to a new area because the man-eating tiger frightened the people so much. Because there are far fewer tigers today, man-eating tigers are now very rare even in India.

As tigers are difficult to study in the wild, little is known about their mating and reproductive behavior. We do know, however, that the tiger and tigress come together briefly

when the female is in season. Scientists do not know just how long this "season" is. Some say it is as short as two weeks, others think the "season" may be as long as four months.

A female tiger can have young when she is three years old, and can then produce a litter every two years. The female in the photograph above is pregnant. You can see her enlarged belly and mammary glands.

The litter, usually three or four cubs, is born fifteen to sixteen weeks after mating. Sometimes only one or two cubs are born. Occasionally there may be as many as seven.

The cubs are born blind and helpless. Cubs weigh about 1.5 kg. (3 lb.) and look like large kittens. The tigress hides them in a place safe from predators — perhaps in a cave, under a fallen tree or log, or in a dense patch of grass.

The cubs spend most of their time sleeping and suckling milk from their mother. They grow rapidly. Their eyes open after one or two weeks. They can only see things near to them. In the first month of life they increase their weight four times. By the age of six weeks they are having their first meals of meat (*above*), but they take milk from the

mother until they are about six months old.

From time to time during the first few weeks the tigress leaves her cubs to go hunting. They stay hidden until her return. When they are about ninety days old she takes them for a stroll. Then they begin to accompany her on hunting trips. They must obey their mother and keep well hidden. By this time some of the cubs may have died. The cause of death is unknown in most

cases. If food is short, weak ones will die of starvation. It is probable that jackals and hyenas prey on newborn tiger cubs. Usually no more than one or two reach adulthood.

In this photograph the tigress has killed a young calf. She is carefully watching her surroundings. She does not see the photographer, who is hidden from view. When she is satisfied there is no danger she makes a low, coughing call. Out of the undergrowth

comes her young cub. Together they feed on the dead calf. The cub at first learns how to feed by trial and error. At first it will try to open the prey in all the wrong places. The tigress, as is usual, has started her meal at the rump (*above*).

At seven months of age the cub is already trying to kill its own prey. The cub in this picture (*right*) is half-grown and about eighteen months old. Cubs stay with their

mothers until they are at least two years old, learning the techniques of survival.

This tiger is wild and free. Will such tigers be saved? If the tiger becomes extinct, the world will have lost one of its most magnificent animals. One or two races of tiger will without a doubt disappear. However, strenuous efforts to preserve tigers are now being made by the World Wildlife Fund, some zoos, and by the governments of countries where the tiger still lives. We must hope that enough is being done to ensure the survival of these splendid wild animals.

Glossary

ALBINO An animal born without coloring in its hair or skin, so that it is white rather than its normal color.

BINOCULAR VISION Animals with forward facing eyes (such as tigers, monkeys, lions and human beings) see two overlapping images of an object at the same time, one image from each eye. This binocular ("two-eyed") vision enables distances to be judged accurately.

CAMOUFLAGE Concealment of an animal by its shape and color which blend with its background.

CARNASSIAL TEETH Cheek teeth in the side of the jaw that act like the blades of a pair of scissors and enable meat to be torn into small pieces.

CARNIVORE A meat-eating animal.

DOMESTIC ANIMAL An animal that has been tamed and bred under human control.

EXTINCT   No longer existing; died out.

NOCTURNAL   Active at night time. Many animals feed and hunt during the night.

PREDATOR   An animal that hunts and eats other animals.

PREY   An animal that is hunted by a PREDATOR for food.

PUGMARK   The footprint or paw print of an animal.

RUFF   Ring of fur around an animal's neck, or a ring of feathers around a bird's neck.

TERRITORY   An area in which an animal feeds and roams, and which it defends against others.

WORLD WILDLIFE FUND   Organization that works to save animals that are in danger of becoming EXTINCT.

Further reading

Baumann, Charly. *Tiger, Tiger: My 25 Years with the Big Cats*. Chicago: Playboy Press, 1975.

Burton, Maurice and Burton, Robert, editors. *The New International Wildlife Encyclopedia*. 21 vols. Milwaukee: Purnell Reference Books, 1980.

Mountfort, Guy. *The Vanishing Jungle*. Boston: Houghton-Mifflin Company, 1970.

Sankhala, Kailash. *Tiger!* New york: Simon and Schuster, 1977.

Singh, Arjan. *Tiger Haven*. New York: Harper and Row, 1973.

Picture Acknowledgements

Ardea, 32-3, 37, 44, 47, 49; Ron Boardman, 43; Frank W. Lane, 38; Natural History Photographic Agency, 11; Picturepoint, 5, 41; and the Zoological Society of London, 7, 9 and 40. All other pictures from Bruce Coleman Limited by the following photographers: Jane Burton, facing p.1, front cover; Bruce Coleman, 4, 42; Alain Compost 10; Eric Crighton, Mary Grant, 12-13, 15, 22-3, 27, 29, 35, endpapers, back cover; Peter Jackson, 17, 21; Gordon Langsbury, 25; Hugh Maynard, 28; Dieter and Mary Plage, 31, 34, 45, 46; G. D. Plage, 16, 18-19, 26; Mike Price, 24.

Index